AMORE FATIGUE

RYAN MORROW

Copyright © Ryan Morrow

"Amore Fatigue"

Credit and Deep Thanks to the following people:
Nickalaus McGee: God-tier Cover Art
Mitch Green: Mastermind of overall Design and Formatting
Chris Cole: Dope Photography

A Special Thanks to Sir Adam Bolts for the incredibly thoughtful forward to this book. You have resurrected my believe that life is filled to the brim with beautiful synchronicities. You just have to be willing to receive them.

Forward

"All, save I, were at rest or in enjoyment;
I, like the arch-fiend, bore a hell within me,
and finding myself unsympathized with,
wished to tear up the trees,
spread havoc and destruction around me,
and then to have sat down and enjoyed the ruin."
Mary Wollstonecraft Shelley, *Frankenstein*

Once I finished Ryan Morrow's *Amore Fatique* I poured myself a drink. And then another. What you have in your hands will bludgeon you no matter your experience or lack thereof; running the gauntlet of these following pages will leave you hurt, longing, sick, and *able* to expiate your crimes of the heart, every phrase a different weapon held by the hands of others and your own with an intent to ignite the gossamer netting of your truth, to detonate the nest of your complacency, to force your gaze upwards toward the tympanum above the reality you have accepted, where rest the timeless semiotic manifestations of those who have braved the contemplation of love. Here it is braved. Imperious LOVE; love diminished, neglected; eyes-glued-to-the-door-love, for sometimes they open. But this you hold is not hope. It is an exegesis of a life who wrote their vows to beauty and love on the ephemeral skin of another.

You will take part in your own autopsy here, and you will be reminded of things. You will have to sew yourself together again afterwards–needle and thread, stitch by stitch–with the knowledge of your pain and the pain you have caused others in the pursuit of love or its fata morgana. Because of these poems you will have to confront your stories.

Once, sleeping in a yurt without electricity tucked into the forests of Allaire State Park, New Jersey, 6 miles from the Atlantic ocean, I was visited by a ghost.

I awoke to soft rapping at the door around 2 in the morning. I opened it with more curiosity than fear. Standing in the weatherless forest before me, slightly bioluminescent in the total darkness of the woods, was a young woman in a white dress. Her brunette hair hung past her shoulders over her slender frame, little braids woven amongst the flowing waves of locks. Her eyes were full of longing and sadness and excitement in one gaze from two striking eyes. Not the eyes of some terror. They were eyes buoyed upon a still lake of promises kept. She took my hand.

"Where have you been? I've been waiting for you for so long." (I can still hear her voice.)

She led me slowly through the woods toward a small circular clearing. Along the perimeter of the clearing I could make out human forms, cloaked shadows, hoods drawn and robes obscuring their arms and feet–if they had any.

In the center of the circle was a stone ambo, more neolithic than catholic, and a large, leather bound book was placed on top, opened to what appeared to be the middle. I do not recall the language although I do clearly remember the black ink of the lettering on its tanned pages. The robed figures standing near the perimeter of the circle inched forward in unison as she placed our hands on the book.

"Now I can show you the power," she spoke, as the book became alive with fire, writhing around our entwined fingers without pain or melting of skin. We locked eyes above this conflagration, solemnly.

For the next while–the canvas of our art having rebelled against the waking frame of time the moment I had first opened the door to her presence–she showed me the power, how to use it and how it uses me, together. We were wed this October night in the forests of New Jersey over a burning tome with a host of robed figures as our witnesses. I was returning to or from something, and had never spoken a word.

The next morning I attended the wedding of a good friend, and upon returning to Iowa, after having spoken with a few friends and locals at the afterparty about my experience, and reading the material available I could find considering the history of Allaire, I learned the area is haunted by a ghost called the "Woman in White." It has been seen by many, though usually at a distance. I was completely baffled. This situation went far beyond me, a one-off, a one night stand. This was something deeper.

I was told the Woman in White had been engaged to be married to a sailor who had left on an ocean voyage never to return. She had pined and waited like Gaud for Yann in Loti's *An Iceland Fisherman*, keeping her vows to a man who had married the sea in a ritual of death instead of her; news of their elopement never reached shore, so she kept hope one day he would return to her and she would be able to present herself to her lover as if time had stopped when he had left that fateful day. However, time continues, and the tenderalls of tuberculosis pulled the air from her sails and drowned her on land.

Did I share some resemblance to her lost love? Was time and place the reason she had brought this ritual upon *me*? Had I manifested this with my own desires and curiosity? Did she love me? Was she previously human or a part of something else? I was (and still am) married, and worried there might be some type of repercussion to this polygamy. There was.

It took many forms. Nightmares to begin. Nightmares spilling the banks of anything I had previously experienced. My body broke out in the most horrifying rash, lasting for weeks after returning home. From my neck to my toes were raised islands of torture that shook my entire nervous system when touched. My vertebrae in my neck exploded and I received a spinal fusion. Legal trouble without reason or proof. Our niece–who was four at the time–came over to our house. She hid behind her mom's legs while we were speaking in our dining room, and then pointed and said, "Who is that standing behind you?" Our life had been upturned by whatever this love was becoming. I would wake and see snakes slithering all over the bed, floor, and walls.

One night, shortly after our first child was born, I heard a noise downstairs in the middle of the night. I followed it. In the living room stood the Woman in White, although this time she was wearing a dress of jealous yellow. In her hands she held a family picture of us. She turned to face me. Her face did not look as it did the first time we met. This time she was upset, and at the moment I thought it was a look of hatred, but now I am not sure. Perhaps it was...

The next morning I compared calendars and realized last night was two years to the day (and possibly hour) we had first met in the forests of Allaire. Our anniversary.

Thankfully, the experiences ended with the dawn (at least I believe), and this is the first I have written about them. Maybe our family picture finally made her give up the ghost. I make an effort not to conjure this powerful, abandoned woman enslaved to a love that never was.. However, *Amore Fatique* unlocks the cabinet where skeletons sleep, and it will unlock yours, "for this is the earth's oldest ballet," and we all know the danse is macabre.

Morrow's writing has always captured the interplay between passion and obsession, possession and the possessed, cosmic freewill and enslavement, beauty and death, prostrating himself before paradox while transcending binary frictions. In *Amore Fatique* these motifs and style are present. The most striking difference, however, is in this work we have the author embodying Marina Abramović in *Rhythm 0:* The 72 objects are present but the audience has become only one, the one who uses all the tools available to keep the joy of love illusive by applying humiliation, confusion, and torture. There is no crowd to intervene when the loaded pistol is placed at his temple.

Although there are sardonic poems and moments sharing the stage and spirit of Wylie's *Generation of Vipers*, the focus here is not to react or be surprised by the stupidity of others. One line sums it up quite nicely: "The healing does the teaching / but the pain gets all the attention." The attention to detail considering the pain of all who travel the crosswinds of love spirals into madness, because "all the words in the universe / are futile and impotent / before Fate's crooked smile.". Do passions become love or does love itself as cosmic force produce passion as an aftertaste, a hint of ambrosia and precursor to insanity if followed into stygian depths? But here and there are pleas for a marooning loss of cognition imbued with enough disorientation to excavate the titan of love from its vertebral throne. Inebriants help, but "Time like a thief - steals our progress / rearranges the furniture / puts our head upon the block / and executes our sweet sweet intoxication." Even battering the brain cannot alter the sane reasoning screaming a love can leave but you are forever changed by it. It renews in this way. You cannot call it unrequited love. The process of becoming this type of love can be best understood in the field of virology.

However, there are no victims here, no woe is me, just a song as old as time with an individual who has become a reverberating conduit for this funeral dirge against their will, an argonaut plunging endlessly inward so they can tell us the tale. And to do this, they must survive. These words before you are not Goethe's *Werther*. There is resilience submerged in the deepest of murk. "Lilacs in-doom" instructs one on how to experience beauty; "God is an Animal" showcases overzealous expressions of love need to be examined before they are assumed to be well received ("I learned long ago / that the balance comes - / from letting go / of just / the right / Things."); "Be Damned" observes the tenacity of a flower growing through the cracks of a sidewalk, encouraging the reader to "bloom while you still can / concrete or consequence - / be damned."

I am in no way saying this is a self-help book. It is a book exploring through macro and micro lenses the unraveling of a person who had a love and lost it. But if I took anything from the pages you are about to read, I would say, "I know deep in my heart / there is no such thing / as *nothing* / not anymore." Even in the void of despair, remember to breathe.

-Adam Bolts, Cedar Falls, Iowa, July, 2024.

"Love is self-mastery, the power to understand, the ability to smile at sorrow. Love ourselves and our fate, fervent acceptance of what the inscrutable has in store for us, even when we cannot fathom nor understand it – that is our goal"

– Hermann Hesse –

"Beauty! Terrible Beauty! A deathless goddess – so she strikes our eyes"

– Homer –

"They fear love because it creates a world they cannot control"

– George Orwell –

"The Fates lead him who will; him who won't they drag"

– Joseph Campbell -

INDIVISIBLE

Come with your beautiful wrath
come with your certitude
Bring forth your patient severity
in waves of sweet absolution

Pounded and pushed
washed and rinsed
rain down
until we are convinced

Come with your feminine mastery
come with your cleansing
Take away all that doesn't belong
as we watch the ritual unfold

Gnaw and wither
erode and decay
this is the Earth's
oldest ballet

The molecules of life
also bring the flood of death
In the eye of every storm
a still and quiet breath

Eternal elements
wind and water - fire and earth
A choreographed dance
from extinction - than back to birth

The present moment is a constant gift
a readymade revelation
set upon the ruins of the past
If nothing else - allow yourself this
one first and last sensation

Clotho

TIED TO THE TRACKS

I feel it both ways
all-ways
my scars burn
with bright memories
a heart crowded
with the vice of obsession

I am tied to the tracks
of beauty's power
and the train is coming fast as fate
I am a captive to a hunger
only one soul can satiate

waiting for annihilation
like a dog for a walk
blissful and oblivious

mountains in the way
of a simple kiss
invisible vampires
make hideous faces
in the bedroom mirror

it shoots through me
like a fever dream
like a wave of amphetamine
an overwhelming euphoria
to feed upon
to become
to die in
this moment

substance and meaning
so elusive
so unimportant
pleasure and orgasm

so easy
so tangible

master of denial
lord of depravity
king of illusion
unworthy of such immaculate skin
drowning in the perfection of lust

overflowing fountains
flooded synapses
maximum ejaculations
a resurrection each night

if only I could speak
if only I knew the words
to break the spell of addiction

just beyond the gate
protected from
this war to come

a tongue held down
by this angel's might

eyes blinded
by this angel's light

love enslaved
to my angel's delight

SOUL'S ABSINTHE

I remember now
what it was I was going to tell you
on that night
with the crooked moon
smiling down
one too many
vodka sodas
floating 'round

I remember building it all up
in a grand crescendo
flailing and dancing about
like I held some secret key
as if it might just kill me
to not set it free

the heat of the moment
gets inside your cells
and pushes out
it lights a fire
behind your eyes
illuminates the truth
reveals the heart's prize

intoxication is a kind of magic
where only certain things are possible
intoxication of *any* kind
of flesh - of drink
of words - of scent
even of absence
you have always been
my soul's absinthe

it's sometimes too easy to discard
the *miracle*
to relinquish the revelation

upon the dawn
when we're no longer
at the pinnacle
and the rush has gone

but when it's being born
burning bright in your hand
or running down your hips
it's oh so precious
caught between our lips

as near as near can get
to divinity
knowing now that I was all yours
and you were all mine

I remember now
what it was
I was going to tell you
but I think I'll keep it here
a little while longer

like a silent song
held in the heart –
even though I know
you've known
the words all along

HUMBLED TO TEARS

Overwhelming love
cripples the heart
and destroys the beholder

Pure adoration
paralyzes the tongue
and defies all logic

Immaculate beauty
can betray the will
and drive you mad

I am humbled
to the point of weeping
by her tender authenticity

I crawl through
hot coals just to
ease this intensity

Love is a myth
always coming to an end
and always being reborn

They never tell you
how truly hard it is -
to stare directly at angels

BREAKFAST IN BEDLAM

I crack the yolk of my anxious mind
overtop the morning stillness

I pour the blood of my troubled heart
into the black depths of a coffee mug

The fruits of someone else's labor
ripen as they meet my tongue

Spices from every corner of the Earth
awaken and trigger a chemical cascade

Sustenance like an atomic military
begins its siege into the bloodstream

ATP warriors all lined up and ready
to sacrifice themselves once more

Prepared for nothing in particular
and yet anything - that might come along

Such power in this hour after dawn
vibrating electrons - each their own paragon

Respiration metronome
floods the castle dome

Begin organic light show
biological workflow

Batteries and engines
hormones and endorphins

Survival addiction
Cosmic contradiction

Equilibrium friction
Fact at war with fiction

Temporal sand grains ever falling
Some cryptic purpose always calling

A mind now ready for life and one's fate
It's just past 8 a.m. here at infinity's gate

YELLOW CAKE

I want you to pose
for this apocalypse
while I write prose
upon your immaculate hips

You are so radiant
with Chernobyl glow
just relax - while I
chain-reaction flow

I'll be the mastermind
you're the plot of a lifetime
we can fuck until we go blind
just promise you'll stay mine

Our minds lost up in a mushroom cloud
our hearts drunk in the gutter
we've ran out of sins - we're way past seven
no candle left to burn – so we just sputter

Something about death and time
Something about beauty and a rhyme
Something about a pit -
from whence no one can climb

This love is an atomic bomb
that I'm begging you to ignite
right here - right now – a burning psalm
die in your arms - I just might

Once in a generation
with a bit of luck and a stiff drink
you can catch love by the tail
but you gotta' be quick
and don't you dare fucking blink

HOME

that old love
that past love
that was no love at all

that was but a straggler
a stray
some kind of imposter
wearing familiar colors

a shade of truth
a flickering simulation
a painting on the wall
that's not quite right

something remains missing -
in absentia

you will know true love
when there are no more pieces
left to search for -
pine for

the puzzle box of questions
will be empty
and your heart
will be stuffed full

there will be nothing left
to ache for
instead you will ache
to give it all away

you will know true love
because it will be the final piece
the correct piece
that found its way home

it will not only
complete the picture -
but make it a masterpiece

GRATITUDE IN CHAINS

In many ways
I'm still terrified
to write my first true line

and there it is
the pause
a studder-step
hesitation *marks*

the fact is
I'm completely broken
by beauty
consumed
by the possibility
of being inadequate

I'm useless
in the full radiance
of her gaze
just a mayfly
smashing against
the streetlight of love

always shimmering
upon the surface
is the purity of surrender
a fleeting innocence
a convincing illusion

paradox rules our lives
never knowing
which path to travel
the blessed always
dancing with the damned

gratitude is tricky

because you never dare
get used to it
for then it will
cease to exist

passion persists
only when it teeters
on the brink
of extinction

each passing moment
more precious
than the last

WINDOW MEDITATION

I see a light on in the building down the street
it's the top floor of an apartment building
I can just make out the shadows of a couple
moving and shifting on the walls

I wonder to myself
are they making love
are they fighting
perhaps plotting a murder
would they rather be doing something else?

I watch as cars fly by - down below
every single one in a hurry
breaking the speed limit
their faces staring at phones
or eating cheeseburgers

Where are they all going?
Where did they come from?
I wonder what would happen if they all
just kept driving in a straight line

I look at the city skyline in the distance
its twilight and the sun is shimmering
off all that metal and glass
I see the idea of a civil society
what came first this diorama or the world?

is there direction or intention to any of this?
is there any way to alter course?

I sit here and wonder
what free will
has to do with love

FALLOUT

soul like a radioactive core.
in meltdown.
mutating. shapeshifting.
glowing with ripe death.
reeking of solitude and
the perfume of desperation.
a life that oozes
beneath the floorboards.
never to be seen again

taking down the medicine
like poisoned ambrosia.
a pill too big to swallow.
receiving wisdom from
the dead and clinically insane.

heart like a psychopath.
on Lysergic Acid Diethylamide.
always so absolutely sure
of what it needs.
screaming with the unbearable joy
of its depravity.

making musical instruments
out of skeletons
drug from dark closets.
sharpening them
into sacrificial weapons.
fashioning golden halos
from polished shit

a mind like a mythic monster
feasting. destroying.
never satisfied.
creating its own universe
to destroy.

I watch you watch me.
wither into bliss.
I close my eyes and imagine
that truth really exists.
I let time unfold
and take what it needs.
there's only one certainty.
everything bleeds.

RATIONS

Writhing with her essence
swimming in a carnal perfume
thrashing in this beautiful curse

I consume my rations
of immortality
kiss by poisoned kiss

Utterly vanquished -
consummated by her flames
I have made a healthy sacrifice
to love's great fire

Grain by infinitesimal grain
between our fingers slips
trapped eternally by our lips

Death is an immaculate woman
carved out of wet stone
dripping with bliss and chaos

she advances her position
each time you dare
to look away

In this terror I am set free
and in freedom I create
a prison for my soul -
to forever hold

THE POLAROID

I keep an adorable
miniature Polaroid picture
of her and I
in my wallet at all times

as if there was a war going on
and it reminds me of home
or peacetime

and in a way there always is -
a war going on

but love - true love
makes any war worth fighting
or at least it used to

in the polaroid
we are embracing and smiling
we both look so happy
and comfortable

we defied the odds
we marched on
even though the world was on fire

it was a frozen joy
but one with incredible power
albeit not invincible
I've since learned -
nothing is

I see the flames of fate
licking at the edges
of our Polaroid

and my heart
is once again being drafted
back into the muddy trenches

POUR THE ABSINTHE

In a room all alone
hunched over a pulsing machine
the burning queen
a death to write me clean

An alter like a woman
pleading for pleasure
yearning treasure
fate pulls our strings to measure

Touch me
Use me
Explore me

A bright white landscape
smoldering with temptation
a dance of sensation
pulling us toward a worthy cremation

Pour me the absinthe
art and love take bravery
a kind of sadistic slavery
face the bliss - even when it's unsavory

Slay me
Entertain me
Be one with me

Give me truth neat in a shot glass
I'll risk the fatality
a foil to banality
defy this persistent duality

Give me death at my peak
don't let me linger past my time
even love can be a crime
ease the blade with clever rhyme

Rattle me
Consume me
Remind me

MEGA-PINT

Never finished
only abandoned

A constant battle
of shifting shapes

A wicked dance with
gorgeous ghosts

There is always the
terrible threat of evolution
a pale promise of perfection
an endless shattered reflection

All art must be tested
in the fires of oblivion

All wisdom comes after
the journey into exile

The forbidden fruit -
a trick or a prize?

How terribly boring Eden
must have been
without its garden visitor

How pedestrian our angels
without their chosen fall
evil against all that is banal

Let's drink each other's blood
and Save Jesus the trouble
one MegaPint at a time

FLICKER

Strung up – like used and abused
Christmas lights
a few still flickering - as if laughing

Strung out - on dreams of rapture
it was never enough - to keep me high
How do the others believe - so easily - the lie

Sure - when it's all going your way
it's as easy as ABC/123
no need to kneel down and pray

But come the tempest -
where do your powers of manifestation go?

Come the rocks in the shallow water –
where does your resilience run to?

Beat down - by Lady Fortune
holding back the odds
no such thing as luck – only dead gods

Filled to the brim - with vacancy
nothing enters and nothing leaves
yet things go missing – tiny thieves

How could it be any other way?
Do the Fates change their mind?

Do we ever really get what we want?
or do our lives simply wear down -
upon the stone of circumstance?

Carved up - into infinitesimal pieces
too small to count - too small to comprehend
destined to descend

A heart laced - with *hope*
but dying from the poison
all the same

DEATH MUSE

Please don't pray for me
for I have nowhere left to go
and no place I must forever be

After this is all through
that's a wrap - a sweet finality
no solution – no grand clue

No need to fear - nor weep
I ask you to just let it all be
I had all I could sow and surly reap

I loved it all - even the pain
the quality of experience reigned
Life after all is but a beautiful stain

All the elements raged deep in my heart
as they did in space and will once more
in some distant sun - until torn apart

Death is not a devil but a *muse*
at once horrifying and beautiful
something to cherish and to use

Do not become callous - nor immune
bathe in this moment just as it is
be engulfed and in the flames commune

Strip life naked - before it is erased
in the end - burden and bliss will weigh the same
Death holds Love – like the apple was *laced*

MADNESS SET FREE

When passion over-ripens in the bottle
and love comes gushing out
When the crimson rose on your walk home
becomes a neon sun of romance
it is there you will find the purity of life - laid bare

As the face of your personal angel
stares at you from the center of your soul
As she grips your mind and sinews alike
capturing your very essence in her mouth
it is there you will know the truth of *surrender*

Love is but madness set free!
or is madness just love unchained?

If only we could glimpse ourselves
from just behind each other's eyes
If only we could savor these moments
like so much dandelion wine
it is there we just stand a chance
at understanding our fate

As divinity is made flesh and fever
in the space between our bodies
As all doubt dissolves in writhing action
heaven becomes a place for all good heathens
it is here that our egos are finally destroyed

Is not love a kind of insanity?
or is insanity just a means to escape love's spell

GERMINATE

It's been raining non-stop for weeks now
a relentless shower gushing from the sky

the water falls to the Earth and then sinks
deep down into the black soil
finding its way into every crevice

I too have been penetrated by the deluge
I too like the dirt –
soak up and consume every drop

something within me germinates
and gracefully pushes up from all my loam
my silent and patient gloom

these invisible cycles transform
small biomechanical wheels turn
a pendulum pivots and returns

a tiny thing awakens
and starts to scream

TANTRIC RITUAL

Somewhere in the back of my mind
the muse is naked and stretched out long
she is eating exotic fruit
the juice dribbles in long streams
over her plump breasts and down
through her immaculate thighs

She is moaning low
or perhaps singing
a bittersweet song of love
Is it desire that burns in her?
or just endless curiosity

Too many days and precious nights
I have ignored this gorgeous creature
that brings such pleasure to my soul
that shines and blossoms -
that transforms any leaden moment into gold

It is not out of malice or spite
that my eyes divert from her light
It is not jealousy nor envy
that my hands remain still -
It is but the seed of fear

I've stood stagnate for too long
the seed cracking open
fed by my indecision - it has become a tree
a force that keeps the door to her chambers
hidden and secure

yet she is always there
wrenching upon my awareness
her body all but begging for attention
aching for my touch
all but ripping my heart from its flimsy cage

and like some tantric ritual I wait
for that magical howl to sound
for the silver light of the moon
to infect my veins
and when the electrons overcome the sky
I will strike like lightning
splitting the tree of fear in two
and dive head long into her eager arms

blood and ink will fuse
love and lust will become indecipherable
science and art shall consume each other
and all will be *forgiven*

CONDUIT

To be completely honest -
I never learned how to write

I just allow the words to pass through me
to *use me up*

I choose not to stop the bleeding -
once it has begun

I've never had any special talent
or known a secret path

I become the conduit -
for languages
I've yet to learn

discovering sweet melodies
within the cacophony
of anguish

I seek no immortality
I wish only - to continue to resonate
with that golden chord
strung up in the center of her cavity

I am but a bottle of spilled ink
upon her silken canvas
desperate for meaning
yearning for purpose

DNA

Despair and hope
twist and coil
'round each other
like two snakes
caught in an eternal dance -
a perpetual love trance

They bite and kiss
wretch in bliss
bound to each other
expand and constrict
trapped like an addict

Each injects the other
with its own kind of venom
in sacred balance
each is the antidote
for the other

Each injects the other
poisoned and cured
in sacred balance
death holds the key
to life's sweetest mystery

AVALANCHE

A few nights inside a foreign city
can give the heart enough fresh blood
to paint every stale wall of our malaise

even the sudden rain shimmers bright
saturating this wilderness with a tasty mystery
flooding these hollow streets with curiosity

the hips push with greater enthusiasm
past the luscious gates once held shut
a golden light now spills out in earnest

weird fruits like sweet candy
our tired flesh feels like new satin
desire becomes a wildfire in a dry-woods

a couple of nights beneath strange stars
can induce the tongue into frenzied dance
singing the poetry of fallen angels

thunder cracks open an autumn sky
like an ancient book in the mind's eye
resurrecting the epic story - back to life

now the lips quiver with slow anticipation
meeting like plump overripe cherries
splitting apart to reveal liquid dreams

drink down the poison like cheap Thai rum
intoxication is a kind of divinity – while it lasts
our passion has become an avalanche
once begun – refuses to be stopped

FUSED

I endure these small agonies
these tiny terrors and casualties
they only hurt a bit
and disappear – like spit on the pavement

they are but little hills to climb
and the valley below is prime
where the wildflowers bloom
hell recedes - from your womb

that is where we lay and thrive
where we truly feel alive

We were once perfect strangers
ignorant to love's dangers
and now when we kiss
it is madness – it is bliss

I feel as if we have fused together
like hot tar and chicken feather
two halves to the same burning sun
there's nowhere left we could run

our time apart only intensifies
solitude - all but purifies

I have become some crawling infinity
you are my destination - pure affinity
there is something calling in your eyes
I'm well on my way – to that sweet demise

GHOSTS

Love is a kind of haunting –
when it's not firmly
in your grasp

it hides in the shadows
and plays tricks
on you

it dances and shimmers
in the corner of your vision

whispering sweet nothings
into your ear

A ghost of itself -
it's only as real
as you make it

one day it's here in your arms
a heart beating hot blood

the next day
it has vanished

just an outline of a person
beneath stained white sheets

LOVE'S MOLD

And just like that
in an instant –
the rose upon my open grave
blossoms in full

the seed within my heart
awakens
and cracks the stone wide

A fire thought extinct
roars up with radiant fury
from the tiniest of embers

Upon my last breath
salvation is seized
from her moist eager lips

Teetering upon the brink -
I cast away all my trivialities
revealing the throbbing marrow
beneath

I drink down her powerful elixirs
letting them revitalize my flesh

I inject her perfect poison
straight into my soul

I am not reborn
but rather recast
in love's mold

I never actually died
only shed the past
like a viper

I was never truly lost
because now I am right
where I need to be

SHEDDING S(K)IN

New radiance creeps
up a dusty spine
photons seeping in
to bring the corpse alive

I look back on my life
as if it was all a bad dream
I can no longer remember
who I thought I was

Fresh luck pours out
like blood from a sacrificial lamb
chance favors the most charming
but also the most wicked

I gaze upon my life
like shed skin – or an old husk
I can't remember
what I once was

Pristine passion pulls the heart
from its rusted cage
love is now as endless
as the desert sands

Life is a series of resurrections
every moment - a new story
I just can't seem to remember
how this one ends

SORROW WAITS

Beauty
has been atomized
inhaled
like silken mist

while the barbarians of desire
pummel their way to bliss

She walks
into every room
like a dragon
of fear and fire

she leaves on bolts of thunder
turning you and me both - into a liar

As lonely as
the new moon
hidden like
a secret told too soon

sorrow waits like a heart-attack
to transmute our lead to gold

LITERATURE OF LOVE

The pleasure I find in bookstores
is a delicate and often
delicious affair

on occasion I find exactly what I need
but not without a deep stare
and a touch of despair

but it pales in comparison
to browsing your glorious bush
of pubic hair

I have learned enough between the pages of a book
but so much more in the library between your legs –
I swear

like an ancient text you are so rare and raw
at every turn my heart –
you manage to repair

and to the last drop I drive to find the cliff
to the bottom - to the end - to some abyss –
devil may care

the insanity of love and wisdom is what I seek
no words - no meaning - only sweet death
endless bedroom warfare

there remains no god - no master - only flesh and intent
you will always be my favorite read – my escape
a kind of final prayer

BEGIN AGAIN

There is no salvation to be granted
no validation to acquire
no trophy - no destination

there is only
this moment

not like the one
that came before –
which is already buried

and not like the one
that is yet to come –
which is never promised

there is only
now

a thing that cannot be captured
only observed
and loved into fruition

EVERY HIT AN OVERDOSE

Beauty is a drug
like any other

too much
and the body swells with arrogance
plumps up with a strange invincibility

illusions of utopia dance wildly about
and destroy the simple pleasures of life

the mundane is buried alive
still screaming

dandelions we once made wishes upon
are trampled on the way to a false divine

too little
and the heart withers unable to thrive
decaying into a stone certainty

delusions of dystopia swarm like hungry insects
the future sinks into a black unknown

spontaneity puts on a collar
and obeys commands

the summer rose that appears in your garden
feels like an invasive weed from Hell

Beauty is a drug
like no other

if given - snorted – absorbed – inhaled
explored – consumed – mainlined – fucked
tasted - burned - swallowed

in the appropriate doses

TRICKED

Love is a sort of amalgamation
a symbiosis of flesh and mind
soul and sinew
heart and heartache

Love is an endless war
A battle of agony and bliss
pain and a soft kiss
one must destroy and also surrender

Love is kind of cyclical death
A dance of blessings and curses
poison and cure
truth and magic trick

ETERNAL MOMENT

I ignore the cat vomit on my desk
so I can type these silly words

I look past the night terrors
and the leaking faucet - so I may find peace

Life cares nothing for our preference
for our age, opinion, or circumstance

Another year
same sold fear

One more time around the sun
this moment is all we've won

Life has never been linear
there is no formula, cheat code, or guidebook

Sure you can draw a line from birth to death
but there is no romance - nor humanity in that breath

Life is a dance in fits and starts
a waltz on the cliff's edge

We are all but snowflakes caught in a winter storm
or perhaps the cosmos attempt - at a new art form

Life is an unruly child
we could never hope to control -
or at least not for long

It is indifferent to our capricious desires
we have our fun - but death – it never tires

It walks over our intentions on its way to Rome
and rolls over our grave on its way back home

And yet – Life is *bursting* with love
plump and ripe
with the nectar of experience
a glorious fugue woven into a greater symphony
every cycle another chance to live deliciously

To win we must hear the music - even in the pain
we must surrender to its power and give fate free reign

Life is not tied to the hands of any clock
but it does keep time
with the infinite in mind

A scale of love - balanced by sadness
a relentless beat - of passion and madness

PIGTAILS

She wore pigtails today.

SHE WORE PIGTAILS TODAY!
and it sets off a cascade of warm emotions
wave upon wave of chemical joy

It begins with a simple smile and a kiss
and then quickly blooms like some newly created flower
something utterly unique - pulled from the magma of life
itself

Perfection isn't the right word for this experience
but it's damn close
it requires a word more delicate
more nuanced and sacred

A word that is woven with ecstasy and misery alike
A word that holds space for eternity and doom in the same
breath
A start that never had an ending
before it came into being

You will know it when -
you have it in the palm of your hands, and they are shaking
with elation
when you feel your heart grow to impossible dimensions
It will terrify you when you understand its rarity

You will know it when –
it all locks into place and you become whole
it will click with the sound of home

You will remember all the times it didn't click
or make any sense at all
you will be horrified to imagine life *without* this feeling

You will know it when –
you make dinner together
and somehow it turns out great every time
Michelin Star level in a galley kitchen
even though you're just making shit up

You will know it when –
your days are as easy as a hot knife through butter
but not in the lazy, apathetic way
more like having the right tool for the job
everything superfluous removed
no piece out of place
everything lands where it needs to land

You will know it when –
you laugh at basically everything
and you're each other's biggest fan

Not a second could be wasted
when you spend it with the right person
the person you love most of all

There is nowhere or nowhen
in the history of life better than that moment
those moments of pure euphoria
future memories forever enshrined in devotion

I just love it when she wears pigtails

FLOOD OF FATE

Kneel down all Ye that seek an easy prize
for if it's worth a damn it's worth dying for
Bow before internal monsters that we immortalize
we are but a momentary masterpiece of love and gore

Hear my rant of this earthly delight
of porcelain flesh and a plump behind
of golden apples and Aphrodite's might
a flood of fate to which my heart shall wind

I was never truly lost nor forgotten
rather drowned by meaning and her miseries
forged in the furnace of some goddess gone rotten
engineered by angels falling in my peripheries

A pursuit of happiness and horror on high
a terrible blessing bound to a beautiful curse
To live is to love and to love is to die
in her body I surrender - dissolve – traverse

Trapped by a swarm of infinities
freed by just a few sweet simplicities
How dare you deny me - the love that completes me?

You cannot enslave a man nor a beast
that begs to never be released
What god killing poison sits upon those lips?

I was given an eternal season
loving her gave me every reason
What could be more evil than blacking out the sun?

DANCING LESSON

I cannot help but feel
a pang of sorrow
when I step upon your toes
as we dance wildly through
this profound romance

I stare like a madman
into your delicious
brown eyes
knowing that I both
belong there and
will be destroyed there

Sometimes a thing
just cannot be repaired
and my heart sputters out
in defeat -
another bittersweet
lesson in surrender

When our time is over
and laid to ruin
my love shall still bloom
in a symphony of color
given your hand and
just one more chance
to dance

LOVE IS AN EXIT

When the hounds of hell arrive
at the threshold of your heart
When all of life comes rushing
toward you're tired eyes
you will understand
just how much I love you

I will be *there*
to slay the most hideous of beasts
I will be there
to lay down upon the tracks
and derail the oncoming train

After a hard day's work
and you just want to collapse
At the bottom of a bottle
just before the last drop
you will remember
that I am waiting for you

I will be here
an escape from the mundane
I will be here
an antidote to despair

We no longer need to pretend
that it wasn't much harder before
we can abandon all our hesitation
and embrace this radiant light

It is no longer required
to simply limb towards serenity
we can run at full speed
and fall naked into bliss

you and I
have been made whole
you and I
have finally found our home

love is an exit
from all that
we once feared

LILACS IN-DOOM

Symmetry has betrayed us
our patterns are breaking
and our vision - lies by omission

Beauty is destined
to abandon us all
but fear not
entropy will hold our hand
to the bitter end

Greet your lover's lips
and make contact with their soul
but do not seek their ownership

Frolic and explore
the absurd abundance of nature
but do not forget the changing season

Taste and indulge
experience the wealth of sensation
but stay humble beneath the sublime

Beauty is programmed
to expire in its current form
but it can never be forgotten
nor vanquished
it merely shifts its habitation

Breathe in the fragrance of every lilac
let it swirl into your depths
but allow it to evaporate without remorse

Enjoy the beating of your heart
but with no expectation
for the next to follow

Seek always more understanding
but understand we can never
know enough

Beauty is doomed
to abandon us all
but that does not
alter its value
but rather increases it
a trillion-fold

QUALITY

Abstraction suits me
like a tailor-made monkey suit
I come alive with slow entropy
dissolving myself into myself

I never cared for the concrete
the *certain* or absolute
give me love - hanging by a thread
give me death in every kiss

We are at our best -
when dancing in acid rain
when reality flirts with the ethereal
when you and I suck the entire universe
through homemade plastic straws

Insanity becomes me
as I shed my skin in fits of laughter
I illuminate my own darkness
finding beauty in this curious sadness

I need fantasy to puncture my reality
mortally wound my certainty
give me the strongest dose they carry
save me the last drop of cyanide

We could never stay still for long -
the music always screaming with fury
and a touch of desperation
our nights promising pain
but with plenty of elation
all our gods fell silent
on basement floors ravished into sleep

Oblivion empowers me
like a far-off planet covered in jewels

I squander my creature comforts
doomed to utter extinction

I demand quality in everything
even if it destroys the thing itself
give me authenticity over plastic rapture
give me one great night of your truest self

We did all we could with what we had -
hunted down the paper tiger of permanence
in exchange for something genuine
we conjured the demon of true love
freed it from its cage of perfect madness
we horded moments just to burn
we had our time in the blazing sun
and now our lives remain - all the more radiant

HUNTED

How can anyone possibly live with "no regrets"?
I somehow doubt it – I'm fatally skeptical

Have they never reacted - when they should have remained silent?
never taken the wrong turn home and paid for it dearly?

I'm filled with the stuff
a collection of regrets
a museum of missed opportunities

Since the day she left
I'm drowning in an ocean of them

Why didn't I show more affection
why wasn't I more vulnerable
I should have loved longer – harder

listened far more than I spoke
healed instead of picking the scabs
reached out versus curling in

Instead - I let the days go by
like so many postcards never answered
allowed the best memories to sink into oblivion

Too much complacency - veiled insecurity
not enough cutting loose and just being silly
exploring the wealth of love's oasis

I regret squandering the most precious of all things
for wanting trinkets when atop a mountain of gold

How could I not regret doing more
when was I filled to the brim with love?

They may live their life with "no regrets"
but I remain *hunted* and *haunted* by them

One for every moment wasted
one for every gaze averted
one for every day - she doesn't return

SONNET OF SORROW

The sun comes up with its dependable glory
carving a bright path through dark skies
bathing the turning leaves in a variegated story
making the grass moist as we open our eyes

With casual purpose we rise without the beep beep beep
coffee is made - breakfast is had - the day begins
with level neurotransmitters and a long deep sleep
two lovers kiss and embrace their warm skins

All seems well in the land of love and routine
but somewhere something stirs in subatomic murk
maybe a neutrino passed through and hit the spleen?
or maybe god farted and the world went berserk

Against the heart's will an ominous mood is cast
just like a black cloud that blocks the sunshine
regardless of inner truth my words escaped aghast
the machine of passion sputtering like a sick bovine

And beneath it all just some genetic puppeteer
unbeknownst to the dancing fool below
under the surface of it all a chemical Shakespeare
writing the comedy and bringing the tragedy out slow

On a perfect day - just like today
I wonder if I shall always act this way
regardless of all my love and best intention
would I still fail at giving you my full attention?

INNOCENCE

I have extinguished the quest
for pure knowledge
entombed it in the greater flame
of love's fire

Life had provided a feast
and I became bloated with its delights
gorged - beyond obscene
a blooming target for the vultures
in the desert wasteland

I sought the pleasure
of utter extinction
nailed sorrow to laughter's hearth
while love waited
with it's dark secret

All children enjoy
murdering their innocence
in exchange -
for the prize of new experience

remembered or forgotten
the rabid foam
upon creation's mouth

The suns of yesterday
have all fallen -
nostalgic hearts
reach with neuronal arms
into astral abyss

once created -
love can never be destroyed
only silenced and enslaved

I run through fields
of fiery blossoms
that pierce through the stones
a maze of ruins
an empire collapsed

I have vanquished desire
that had yet to tire
I fed it piecemeal -
to the hounds of circumstance
so that the sleeping dragon
would not stir

I do not believe
the angel shall return
even by pulling down
the very heavens from the sky
yet still – we must try

DYING IN REVERSE

Nothing left to complain about
yet we still could - and often do
find something

to bring the bliss to an end
to impale the perfect stillness
with bit of chaos
to make this joy ride - seem like work

What is this sudden decay?
of all our most beautiful flowers
wilting petals of sorrow
our melancholic progress toward the sea

Let your cravings cave in
Get strong off the burial
of all things superfluous

This existential light
illuminates our fear
our hopes scatter like cockroaches
with nowhere left to hide

It should be enough
yet it rarely is -
there's always a morsel more

to gain or obtain in thinning quantities
to win and devour without ritual
to possess and charm only to forget
and not forgive

What is this forced survival?
hollow statues leaning from neglect
the gold veneer rubbed away
our truth is sinking to the ocean's floor

Allow time to dissolve you
give your body to the elements
make room for the universe to grow
empty inside you

This existential light - illuminates our shame
like filthy bedsheets in the morning light
the persistent stains of a lifetime

ODE TO OUR APOCALYPSE

To reclaim love
from the crumbling cathedral -
this tired dream of dust

To salvage love
from the serrated junkyard -
a malaise of (t)rust

There is such wealth
in all we have discarded
beauty - in the agony
of the brokenhearted

The more our love is neglected
laid to rest in obscurity
the inherent value only grows
pushing its way to purity

The path of nothing resisted
leads to bliss-full unknowns
the path of everything accepted
ends in dirt and bones

Was he merely a drunkard
drowning in booze and delusion?
or was he a wise philosopher
seeing what no one else could

A fool
or perhaps
a timeless lover

Was she just a whore
hiding behind youth and innocence
or was she a genius of the heart
knowing the end before it arrives

An addict
or maybe
the last true romantic

Is tonight the night?
we join our jagged lips
in saliva and redemption
an ode to our apocalypse

CHEERS

I drink
to reappear
exactly where I am.
reborn.

I drink
to arrive
nowhere in particular.
and forget the details.

I drink
to pull time
into me.
and through me.

Pour me another.
Pour me redemption in a glass.
Pour me one more chance.

I drink
out of crippling luxury

I drink
because the past is done.
cannot be undone.

I drink for the *fallen*
I drink for the disillusioned
but mostly -
I drink for me.
(whoever that might be)

I drink
to silence my demons
I drink
to make the last of my angels
smile

I drink
to end the trial.
O' the rapture of denial.

Pour me the last of it.
Pour me out with it.
Pour Pour me.

UNTITLED

Covered in blood
and red lipstick -
this love is a war
of mutual attrition

Wearing each other down
with perfect poison -
our hearts sink
into some sweet devastation

DIRTY MIRROR

She says I should write something tonight
and she's usually right about these things

I woke up today as if someone had exchanged my mind
for another – a strange and foreign one

as if it was swapped out in the night
with a fool's brain - one who hadn't learned his lesson yet

Where did the man go that crawled into this bed?
like complex math equations on a chalkboard -
they've all been erased

I knew things then - just yesterday
everything was bright and crystal clear

Now it's just filth and fog
smeared on a broken mirror

I sense as if I might be trapped - in some sort of loop
a repeating amnesia - a maze without a center

I seem now to be some *approximation*
an estimation of a complete human -
missing a link – with a few bends and a major kink

my mind is a pair of corded headphones – tossed in a bag
no matter how I try - no matter how delicately I place them
when I go to retrieve them –
they are in a hideous impossible knot
all things find their way to rot

My thoughts are now a chaotic jumble
even though they were once sorted and filed away
picked apart and analyzed –
Revelations in the R's

Epiphanies in the E's
Lessons in **Bold** and <u>Underlined</u>

flaws to correct and future goals
ambitious to-do-lists and lofty insights

But alas we drift into sleep
and the disorder slithers in through the keyhole
entropy always finds a way - to our dismay

Time like a thief - steals our progress
rearranges the furniture
puts our head upon the block
and executes our sweet intoxication

We are not yet completely broken –
yet we seem to be doomed to endless repair

We are not completely lost –
yet we are always rerouting our course

We are not utterly confused –
and yet we always forget
just how the story goes

LOVE'S ATRIUM

"It's a quarter past midnight."
she whispers, as the moonlight drips over her
like slow melted honey
made in a queen bee's hive.
Somewhere - where paradise thrives.

I try and act cavalier
but the truth is I'm smitten. Thrice bitten.
Overcome with admiration. Exultation.
Caught in a continuous seduction.

Is it always this radiant in our living room?
In the center of love's throbbing atrium.

The days have been flying by.
Whirling past our silly love-drunk heads.
And at the same time, they've been crawling
like a dry snail across incomplete concreate.

Isn't that neat? The way time can dilate.
becoming almost insignificant.
So untethered to reality.

I'll bet you a gazillion dollars.
I don't make it out of this room alive.
Well ok, I'll survive. but I won't be the same.

That's what happens when a fool like me
stubbled into the grace of an angel. The den of a lioness.
Is reborn in the womb of desire.

Good thing I'm not in a competition
for a perfect ass or unlimited sass.
I have truly met my maker. My proverbial heart taker.

It's moments like these that I think we're all working toward.

secretly pining for. Trading life, time, and money for.
To meet your adversary.
In the form of submissive love.
A battle you can't win. Because you don't want to.

In this realm is the merging of many forms.
boredom and revelation. Bliss and devastation.
Peace and rapture – all fused.

When the chase has subsided. The meal requited.
It is time to savor all of life's flavor.
It is time to discover. And perhaps recover.
All that was lost or hidden.
In love - nothing is truly forbidden.

Love is the grand solvent. Ultimate emulsifier.
The great dissolution of self.
A dissolving of two into one.

I once feared the infinite space of the sublime.
but now what terrifies me - is returning.
to the ordinary mud of time.
(without you).

PULLED THROUGH TIME

It began with an argument. a silly argument.
but then again aren't they all.

Is there ever really "a point."
a destination.
or any ultimate solution.
or is it all so much dust
for the wind to scatter.
flotsam and jetsam for the seas
to disperse our matter.

I know not the answer to this ancient riddle.
I am but a student of its continuous mystery.

Can you deeply care for someone and remain indifferent?
when to push - when to pull.
when to bend to the inescapable.

or should we command our pernicious doubts
to the front lines.
sacrificial pawns for the bullets of desire.

Does not passion tend to root itself in the soil of possession?
in the moment of convulsive catharsis.
at the pinnacle of love's expression.

Does not progress stem from the wanting of betterment?
from the idea that there is something else to strive for.
to drag ourselves through time for.

Can we put one foot in front of the other?
if not for the need to get somewhere – *different.*
than where we are.

And yet upon request one is asked by their beloved
to relinquish the power they once begged to obtain.

to extinguish the flame they ignited with vigor.

it's just a little thing. everything is a little thing in the end.
it's all trivial if you just let it be.
if we zoom out enough.
Is this the game we wish to play?

no one wants to zoom in so much that their world
is split into an endless fractal array of concern.
and petty circumstance.
of nothing but microscopic bugs
turned into Godzilla sized monstrosities.

We must choose our battles.
and yet when does the battle begin.
and does it ever really end.

To win the war
is to stay rent free
in your lover's heart.

Love shall remain the ruler.
even in the wreckage.
even in the ruins of it all.

we shall call it surrender.
we shall call it discipline.
we shall call it *forgiveness*.

Love is death without dying.
an extinction you both ask for.
one you may never return from.

SAME SAME - BUT DIFFERENT

I soil her dress
in a Bangkok hotel

she stains my heart
with her sweet poison

we dance on the beach -
like new cosmic dust

we fuck away our fears -
like Olympian gods

I tell her "I could die happy
right now" and I mean it

she says, "I could kill you,
I love you so much"
and I know she means it

the world is always more delicious
when we taste it together

this wild city continues to close in
but we remain far far away

Lachesis

CONTRADICTIONS

everything - everyone
is so arrogant these days
standing tall and gloating
like so many decorated pigs
before the slaughter

we have forgotten what hubris means
caught in a vice of perpetual screens

winning the genetic lottery
can make you rich beyond measure
but it shouldn't make you cruel
beauty equals riches
while the rest get stitches

we have syphoned out the humility
from what was once our humanity

oceans don't separate much these days
but a few thousand dollars
can make a universe of difference
who really deserves
wealth without limits?

we claim we want equity without lies
yet we continuously vote for injustice - with our eyes

technology feeds upon itself
plugged in and addicted to itself
the ancients are bound and gagged
entombed inside our hard drives
organic-mechanic messiahs
coming every second

we have outsourced our very existence
algorithms rule us without resistance

it pumps through our veins like heroin
it crawls around our minds like cancer
it's in everything – everything new
bitter is the only taste that remains
time stealing our ever-precious grains

NOTHING HURT

There is no forcing it – really
all is just as it should be

the crescendo of a rose
but a moment too late

love that goes stale
like some terrible disease

life is but a dream
you can't quite remember

we slip through time
like snakes between raindrops

we sneak under each other's skin
like slow needles

the healing does the teaching
but the pain gets all the attention

have you ever taken *medicine*
when nothing hurt?

have you ever gotten away with it?
or evaded the trap?

can you imagine all of this -
any other way?

is there any other path
than the exact one we took to get here?

WORM FOOD

I'm a walking dead-man
I died that night
on the couch
just as soon as you said
"I'm leaving you"

Since then I just pretend
that the sun feels good upon my face
that my days are worthwhile
that cooking for one -
is still fun

But I know the truth
and so does the world
I was buried and forgotten
all in an instant
a poet ripe for the worms
a casualty of love
turned into cheap infatuation

Yes, I will survive
and yes, you will thrive
and if we listen to the
therapists, sages, and
motivational speakers
they will all say
"this is an opportunity"
"you will be better on the other side"

Well, that's all fine and dandy
but if this is going to be
a total transformation
a complete resurrection
then I'm going to need
my heart to stop aching

WINTER OF THE SOUL

they continue to bubble up
gush and spew
these little memories - of you

like when you would always try
biting my nipples
and I would uncontrollably giggle
like a child

or when we were both in the bathtub
with flickering candles
your head on my chest
watching shadows dance on the wall
in that beautiful stillness

my hand on your thigh
as we drove into the wilderness
or when we made up silly little songs
for all our furry pets

dancing like crazy people
to Bjork at breakfast
or random cocktail creations
at 3 in the morning

when you would flash me a tit
or moon me through every window you could find
or eating every meal -
as if it was our last

you are the most radiant creature
I have ever known
and I basked in your light
for as long as I was allowed

now the winter of my soul
has begun in earnest
and I cannot help but pray
for one more spring - in your arms

CAN I GET A REFILL

The neighbors are at it again
having a big yard party
mumble rap on blast
joints on puff puff pass
gin with juice - but just a splash

I spot the "peddle-pub"
once again riding around the block
and all I hear is that familiar - yet horrifying
"whooooo whoooo whahooo"
always someone far too excited
about drinking in a giant Flintstone's car
going 5 miles an hour

"The Eagles" band is also in town tonight
their tired worn-out songs
punctuating through the rap
like a stale slow-moving fart
the drunken crowd on wheels goes wild

I can only hope and pray
that there are more human souls
in existence - like myself
drinking alone in peace

more rare creatures
sitting in dimly lit rooms
fighting the good fight
against misery - against themselves
without all the pageantry

I gaze out my window
onto a concrete jungle
and decide to travel inward
into the last true wilderness
to try and make death smile
without ever leaving my chair

ok maybe for a refill

THE DEVIL HIMSELF

Leave these memories
in their cave
of sublimity

let them remain
unfed and unenhanced
fading into the shadows
of the past

Lay at the feet
of all your horrible
mistakes

and tell them stories
with a slow silver tongue

I wait for wisdom
to fill me -
but only hubris arrives
and folly close behind

I resist the temptations
of all my lesser demons
holding out for the
devil himself

I let time stretch
and mutilate my identity
beyond all recognition
this is now
the *new me*

Simply saying we are
Indestructible -
will not prevent
sorrow from taking
what is his

BARBARIANS AREN'T WE ALL

These are the days
I love to hate - the most

the days I feel like
I've got the world upon a string
marionetting
according to my whim

the warm sun beating down
upon our hungover faces
she is my breakfast in bed
can't believe I'm not dead

easy love and endless kisses
too perfect – that's what this is

glorious options
stretched out before us
open and free
untreaded – yearning
to be known and
explored

I'm overwhelmed with
all this pristine landscape

got the booze
got the woman
got the moment in my pocket

the only resistance is me -
against me

these days are the hardest
the hardest - to *finish*
they make me feel

like some kind of barbarian
trudging through a field of wildflowers

every step I take
trampling something beautiful
something precious
making room -
for empty progress
to somehow just maybe –
change her mind

FATE'S FOOL

What does it matter, really?
when it is you - the broken man
against a perfect angel

you the creature
of mistake and misfortune
pitted against the infallible

What can passion change?
What has love to overcome?

the fool shall remain the fool
standing next to the alter -
of radiance

all the words in the universe
are futile and impotent
before Fate's crooked smile

all that was once meaningful and true
becomes so much kindling
for the fire of her disregard

CLIPPED

And just like that
all the significance explodes
vaporizes right before my eyes

years of worship dissolve
and then pool
into the drain

all we have built
so easily wiped from this Earth
in a single renunciation

a beating heart rendered useless
pissed on - as if trash in an alleyway

How is it possible
to have such brilliance wasted
pure radiance eclipsed

an angel's wings clipped -
to stuff a cheap stained pillow

What is it all for?
this mechanism of love
made to shatter and then vanish

years of adoration disregarded
and thrown to the hounds -
of heartache

I am the child of surprise
weeping with a wet diaper
as the world continues
to turn and burn
leaving me with the husk
of true love

MEAL TICKET

Last night - inside the wet heat of passion
I pulled my aching heart
straight from its cavity
and fed it to a siren's depravity

beyond any discipline - spun out of control
I shed my tired skin and stood truly naked
beneath her red atomic sky
in ecstasy - nearly wanting to die

I became a raw feast
fed directly into two starving eyes
one demonic and burning
the other angelic and yearning

demanded from my frame
was the severed head of rage
pulled forth from my soul
was the lynchpin - to my cage

I became a child once more
playing in a sandbox of wonder and awe
amazed at how a single person
can open you wide and change it all

our time together was as full
as a Halloween candy sack
bathing in each other's presence
each moment - a delicious snack

in the end there remains a body of wounds
to remember how good it can get
but never was there an ounce of pain or shred of regret
what I wouldn't give to return − to repeat the threat

LET IT HAPPEN

I sit like a frozen flame
caught between
a teetering choice -
of an immediate ending
and infinitude

I let the moon burn through me
with her wisdom reflected
from an immeasurable past

she glimmers -
and speaks these words

"Purpose waits where the raging river communes
with the stillness of the ocean

when the shadow illuminates
when the silence reveals
when love blooms from heartache

that is when
you will find the strength -
to let it happen"

GOD IS AN ANIMAL

All of life is a kind of burning
of countless chemical fires
that rage and spire - cage and inspire
sputter and spit - just dying to stay lit

God is a filthy animal
with no way to get clean

but there is a way
to bend everything
so that it appears as destiny

there is a way to break anything
to make it immortal

Understand this –
caring too much
will bring you
maximum suffering

caring too little
will leave you
abandoned and empty

I learned long ago
that the balance comes -
from letting go

of just
the right
things

BOUND

fresh ink to stain these vacant pages
bittersweet words to weave us through the ages

deep within the poet's aching heart
pain is transformed into eternal art

dreams mutate to flesh and marrow
beauty is tied to the tracks of sorrow

the muses fall from a graceless sky
but they are pure of soul and cannot die

the truth is not meant to be found
tragedy and comedy forever bound

CHILD OF WONDER

I can hear her high heels
clicking down the pavement
I know she's coming for me – once again

I can feel her approaching- ever closer
with a slow methodical stride
a casual doom
like a razor that splits your skin wide open -
before you feel a thing

I sense her already inside my head
a burgeoning occupancy
a bittersweet dread
like a wound that refuses to close
smiling with pride

All my resistance bleeds out
as a strange wind blows up her little black dress
and gives me a glimpse of paradise
or is just hell - before the fall

My passion is as ripe as a summer berry
wet to the touch – dripping with anticipation
time itself shutters - intoxicated with her radiance
I am a child of wonder in her arms

Every time I come around this bend
it feels just like the first
but I have died so many times now
that we've both lost count

I didn't ask to live forever
but I also didn't promise – I wouldn't beg
for this rapture - to never end

SONG OF THE DAMNED

A once radiant urgency
of creation and passion
to impress and dazzle
to go beyond the limits

is fading and dimming
threatening to flicker out

That once insatiable craving
to swallow the world whole
to grab life by the fistfuls
and toss it casually in the air
life so much cheap confetti

is weakening and growing stale
all too close to complete exhaustion

Like some exotic
dance of death
a warrior's waltz
winding down

the song of the damned
is more beautiful
because it is their last

This melody is not
without its charms
a poisoned apple to the ravenous

Not without its immaculate
bleeding hook
reminding the heart of its glory

but it is a bittersweet kiss
laid to rest

upon the lips of a traveler
with nowhere left to go

A grim love letter
like an iron nail
to finally seal the coffin
of this tired dream

PENANCE

I acted tough for so many years
that I started to believe it
but the truth is I'm not tough -
I'm broken

Riddled with scars
and weighed down by insecurities

The day she left - that raging truth
came rushing back
to flood every crack
to fill every crevice

To once again - take up arms
Crawl back into those deep trenches
of doubt

Now the pressure returns
pushing from the inside
instead of the outside

I know I must change
I must change or I will die -
be unrecognizable to *anyone*

Not just for her
or for what was
but for myself
For the greater good -
for this brave new world

I cannot accept - *that* was my best
that I was at my best
and all is doomed to ruin

Lo! I must believe

that if only these holes were mended
the soul would heal just like a body

That if my transgressions were dragged
into the light and exposed
they would finally be vanquished

Lo! I must believe
that one day sorrow
can deliver redemption

That self-forgiveness
can wash away these stains of passion

My survival depends
on knowing - I could have done better
but I must now serve that love in exile – in chains
with full intent – with unquavering certainty
with the power of a man with purpose
with love still left in his heart

AUTOPSY

Ripped open
and on display
like an autopsy
for all to see

beyond naked
way past vulnerable
stripped down
to the very essence
of my soul

cut by tiny cut
I am revealed
to myself
and to your beautiful
yet terrible
gorgon eyes

once I was whole
now I am nothing
but the stone dust
of your gaze

consumed by an ache
so deep
and so severe
it has become the
fabric of my being

I want only -
to suffer more
if that means
not losing you

FOR BETTER AND WORSE

It's all closing in -
loneliness like a
claustrophobic coffin

It's getting darker now -
the light of love
is flickering out

It feels as though there are
vultures circling in spirals above
just waiting for my collapse
to devour what is left of me

It just doesn't seem real anymore –
any of this
the illusion never sleeps

If what came before
was not what it appeared
then why should what comes next

I'm counting the seconds
until my heart skips
and finally sputters out

My heart keeps howling
for help - for a redo - for forgiveness
but only silence answers

It seems I can no longer
make it better
the best I can do
is to not make it worse

and perhaps
that is enough -
for now

EXPIRED CHAMPAGNE CLUB

You incomplete me
tearing me from the core
making my heart beg
like a common whore

I still wretch from your beauty
vomiting precious moments
chunks of nostalgia
sick with all I told ya

Trapped in cycles and circles
of our endless discourse
memories of our
everlasting intercourse

Death would have been better
more *certain* more severe
I know there is not
and could not be - A *Cure*

I lost you and now
I am lost in turn –
and yet still the heart
does what it must
continues to burn

Building up to imaginary heavens
for some reason -- what was the reason?
collapsing from within
passion has become utter treason

Maybe there is a lesson here
in the mud and shit and pain
in the meantime,
I drink to honor our love
like so much expired champagne

SYMPATHY FOR THE DEVIL

We're in love with our certain doom
At the height of a deep summer bloom

Our adoration swelling like an ocean tide
Upon mermaid's backs we ride

Knowing it might all come to an end
we cannot change the fire we rend

Locked in pure reverie and dreams
Tranquil visions pour out in streams

To touch the threads of pure life
is to cut out your heart with a cosmic knife

I sing in harmony with atomic angels
and howl in excess with demonic bells

Indulge in the Earth's bursting light
Sympathize with the monster's plight

Watch as the rusted chalice overflows
Lean into life's steady persistent blows

RUNNING OF FUMES

On cheap air mattresses
quickly deflating

In desert bungalows
with mice scurrying about
eating our avocados in the night

On the road
in utter silence
On the road
in chaos and euphoria

there is love in there

In crowded gothic theatres
In car crashes
lost in the High Sierra
shivering from the cold

Waiting in lines at venues
and taco trucks
with bloodshot eyes
and exhausted smiles

there is love in there

In anticipation
In the aftermath
down in the abyss

Inside rotting fruit
that you eat anyway
In stale seltzers
the morning after

there is love in there

Hidden in-between
the cheese and mystery meat
of sandwiches
made out of rental car trunks

In stinky kisses six miles in
on a two-mile hike

There is still love in there

At the outskirts of *almost there*
At the perimeter of just about home

In the out of gas at the gates of paradise
the never perfect
but that's what makes it ours

In the you were mine
and I was yours
(but no longer)

There is enough love in there
to last a lifetime

LOVE POEM #99

Love at the bottom
makes you feel tall
Love in a bottle
is no love at all

Love coils tightly around you
yet makes you feel *free*
Love captured -
ceases to be

Love on demand
gives you wings
Love just as easily
clips and kills kings

Love is the answer
To all our silly questions
Love like wildfire
remedies all our transgressions

Love makes the stone
once again movable
Love makes the sadness
in us provable

Love creates in us
something truly beautiful
Love makes madness in us
pure and dutiful

MUZZLED

Somewhere in the wilderness of myself
wolves are being muzzled
trees are losing their leaves
the chloroform of her sad song
lulls my bones to sleep

Tonight my heart has a passenger
and it's pulling the brakes at every turn
depriving my engine of fire
and draining the tank of hope

I know this specter will release me
I know my wolves will hunt again
but under this spell of sorrow
I am paralyzed – unable to break free

If only she would call - out to me

EQUAL MEASURE

The highs burn off in ecstatic demise
the buzz always drowns inside itself
yet her beauty remains – uncaptured
somewhere on the horizon

Oiled skin and wet lips tire in exhaustion
eyes deepen and close with their own weight
yet her charm only grows – insatiable
erupting from below

Peak experiences overflow from our chalice -
yet it is always being drained from the bottom

A flood of memories watching our reflections –
in a shattered mirror

It matters
It matters not
It matters
It matters not
petals plucked from
an imaginary flower

I am a conservationist
preserving the *delight*
alongside this *dread*
they both contain your essence
in equal measure

I wonder if it would feel any different
if we knew all along
that it wasn't meant to last?

METHOD AND MADNESS

I pull these words
from an aching heart
like bodies out of shallow graves

I drag them from their sanctuary
into the radiant sunlight

Wretched and untethered
from their former silence
they writhe and resist
their re-examination

husks of their former ideals
they move - but dance no longer
falling short
of complete re-animation

I push my intent
up the mountain
like a starving mule
whose last meal lies at the top

every step forward toward a void
and away from abyss

This failing machine
sputters out a message
and finds pale meaning
as it approaches its limits

There are no ghosts
only convincing illusions

There are no spirts
only divine intoxication

There are no gods
only theories
that haven't been
destroyed yet

THE CARTOGRAPHER

I feel as though I have mapped out
the landscape of my heart
through our memories –
a sort of retired cartographer

I climbed incredible mountains
far past the clouds
up into the heavens -
just to meet her gaze

I floated down raging streams
into the valleys below
laughing all the while -
no thought of consequence

Remembering days
where we did nothing at all
and others where we pushed the limits -
life was always unfolding

Days of routine
days of magic and mushrooms
all with purpose -
because we had each other

The sun always seems to be shining in my memories
giving warmth and light through it all
the radiance of home
the illusion of permanence

I uncover caves and crevices
each one with their own depth
their own trappings and delights
things with density - but no weight

Little treasures strewn along the way

new recipes - dope music - silly dance moves
flower beds and furry creatures
cunnilingus – oculolinctus – all for us

I feel as though I've traveled
these landscapes for a lifetime
now but foggy dreamscapes
they shall fade but remain mine

I cannot shake that
there was always more to discover
to see - to feel - to understand
to *surrender* to

Now I must let it all go
leave this place of death
and let another cartographer
map their course through paradise (lost)

WE NEED A NEW MYTH

The world is collapsing
imploding in upon itself
and the poets are all too drunk
or high to write it down

We are all drowning
in trivial luxuries
while the ancient heart of Aphrodite
breaks and disintegrates into dust

We are all begging for a morsel
of meaning as we chew endlessly
on the empty carcass of culture

The snake crawls back into its dead skin
and the sun returns to the east
past Eden - past Hell

The blood of forgotten soldiers
still stain the Earth –
bubbling up to remind us
of our hubris and folly

Ancient snow and ice recede
thawing past lovers and beasts alike
No blossoms yet - only seeds
holding dreams of dead flowers

There are no more secrets
only truths to bend and facts to amend
reshaping life like stale Plato
pulled from the floorboards

What we need is someone strong to guide us
to you tell us it's no longer worth the effort
But what we need is not what we desire

yet we cannot change what we truly want

The first kiss is always the last
all moments singular and precious
alive and dead in the same instant

I am convinced of only one thing
true love
is both beauty and dread
in equal measure

THE GODLESS PARTICLE

I dance upon the accumulated graves
of all my former selves
they moan and groan
begging me for forgiveness

I just keep
dancing

Father Time is drunk again
bending linear moments
into hoops and spirals
before he retires to his
bed of nails
where he will weep
and the world will flood in turn

There is a pernicious thought
that has long pupated in my mind
like an exotic bird
trapped in its eggshell – refusing to hatch

I fear what is inside
may have no scale
in which to measure
its preciousness

What if the *quality* of life
is just hubris
disguised

What if we are
but fools of biochemistry
free and yet doomed
blessed but damned all the same

What if we remain inextricably blind

to the glistening truth
at the center of it all
of the cosmos and consciousness

Truth just one more layer down
like endless Russian nesting dolls

Hell has always been
just a metaphor
but its fire - will still consume us all

HAUNTED

I can still hear the melody
of her tireless love
invading my eardrums
drowning out all my useless plans

I wander these haunted hallways
floating from one room to the next
like a dreamer lost in a maze
always in the trail of her sweet perfume

Anticipation of our reunion grows
like a sacred neon rose
outshining all my other thoughts
I think of *nothing else*

The metal of my resistance
melts like butter into her soft
and manicured hands

No armor of mine could ever
withstand the kisses she blows

Her curves and creases seize me
transmuting my sorrow
into erections and laughter

I wait for my tired angel to once again
tumble down from the clouds
and into my open arms

RECYCLED ELEMENTS

We are all grinding and groaning
through the guts of this mad machine
just trying to leave a mark or a stain
a love letter on all that is pristine

When there's nothing left to chase
we are what gets chased - hunted - erased

Our hearts moan from the weight of dust
our souls groan beneath ash and rust

We are but fuel for the space gods of fire
recycled elements for the *afterworld*
watching each-other bloom and decay
waiting as the butterfly awakens and unfurls

A message in a bottle sitting in a dead sea
can't you see it was never about you or me

A shattered mirror spraying legions of her reflection
no more tears just the profound ache of revelation

RECENT HISTORY

I finally changed my phone's background photo today
It was a simple gesture and yet -
it was a crushing blow

Collapsing ever more walls
of a vacating heart
A deconstruction
of the mansion of love

In the photo she was blowing me a kiss
with her big juicy lips

There was a Snapchat filter on
where she was wearing heart-shaped glasses
and in the reflection of the lenses
was my smiling face

Changing the photo felt wrong
sacrilegious even

In that moment
I was the executioner of everything beautiful

If I had my way
I would look at that face for a lifetime

But I did it all the same – erased the reminder
the moment

It turns out healing
is also a kind of destroying

No matter the prize
it shall one day fade
into the greater background.

MIDNIGHT VOWS

Too much optimism
always wounds the muse
and kills our mood

making promises of grandeur
destroys the spontaneity
I beg you – just make a move

Love is meant to be untamed
never caged or fed on a schedule
never put on a leash (unless it's for fun)

I wait like a starving hyena
for her big juicy lips
for her warm embrace
for something new to break my heart

There is never a guarantee in this game
nothing certain – only passion
and nervous dice rolls

all bets made are stacked
against a crooked house
and we always find the limit

we poison each other with midnight vows
we promise that we'll keep
we stain and cut each other like broken glass
artists of a beautiful destruction

I wait like a desperate junkie
for another cocktail
for just one more kiss
for even the slightest chance
and one simple death wish

RATS

Love makes rats of us all
trapped in endless circles
on this wheel of misfortune

Love turns us all into worms
just waiting for the next
falling sacrifice

Beauty is a curse
and I shall reverse its spell
one bloody kiss at a time

BE DAMNED

I walk down 42nd street
nearly every day of my life
and there is always this
tiny purple flower
that relentlessly bursts up
between cracks of concrete

It gives me a strange sort of hope
albeit a sad and feeble one
but just like that little flower
I feel myself pushing -
up through the dirt
and the shit
regardless of the world's boundaries
just to catch a few rays of sunlight

When I do
it always feels divine and
somehow right on time
I become filled by the wild bliss -
of survival
I made it one more day you fuckers!
whoever you are

I move ever-toward the sun
and open sky
the sun is my *god*

just like that persistent flower
(there's plenty of our god to go around)

I feel an innate urge
to display my colors
to fan out in radiant defiance
or maybe a desperate Hail Mary
either way death is coming

and the right time is always now –
to resist

We all know what is
lurking around the corner
creatures with their poison fangs
they come to trample
and destroy our progress

So bloom while you still can
concrete or consequence -
be damned

THE RIME OF THE DROWNED MAN

I bolted upright at 4am
covered in cold sweat from a horrible nightmare
It was the third time this week
proof when the heart is suffering it screams out to repair

In the dream I was lost at sea on a rundown ship
a terrible storm was surrounding
I searched in delirious fits for the one I love
my chest tight and pounding

I looked everywhere while the rain slammed my face
and lightning ripped open a dark sky
Then I heard sounds from the cabin below
they were sounds of wild pleasure not ones scared to die

As I made my way down below, I could feel
Fate's shears closing in upon my thread
Slipping round my neck
holding me up by my lovesick head

Alas she was not there - nor anywhere
and there was nowhere left to search
So I gazed out into the lurching tempest
the center of that black church

In that moment the truth was revealed
a terrifying and brutal truth
There she was - far off on distant shore
made of foam and fury - flesh and tooth

Singing me through another impossible night
calling me back home
I knew I could not reach her alive
it would be as sea and loam

My tears joined the deluge

diluting into the crashing waves
What awaited me was not lips and soft skin
but a bed of salt and water graves

The thing about true love is that it doesn't change
not even after it's mutilated and skinned
It refuses to dwindle or decay
even when shattered and scattered to the wind

Love can only heal and forgive
outliving any pain that it endures - in time
I hope I'm strong enough to forgive myself in turn
with the help of the sea and this bittersweet rime

I will continue to look for her in my dreams
even when it burns all along
'Cause there - I still get to see her exquisite face
and hear her delicious siren song

DRINK THE KOOL-AID

It feels so impossibly good
to be in her presence
to be locked under her spell
to be the prize of something
beautiful beyond measure

I have often wondered why
I don't just give up the act entirely
for this rapture
for this precious escape
for her healing touch

she is a fire without a master
a force without a foil
it's enough to drive you mad

but instead of surrendering
I tried to play it cool
I kept punching in the clock
and putting in the hours
for some paper to burn
for trivial intellectual ghosts

all the while -
she filled my heart to the brim
until it saturated my soul

somewhere in me was a fateful clock
keeping the beat of doom
a metronome taunting -
"nothing lasts forever"

I should have known better
than to swallow the poison of permanence
drink down the Kool-Aid of true love

we've all been through hell
and yet we still expect to be punished
some Freudian complex
of the modern world

our chains fashioned
from the strangest of materials
our prison cell ever shifting
to accommodate our needs

I had paradise purring
like a cat in heat upon my bed
giving me all the attention I could ever need
and yet somehow, I allowed my brain
to silence my heart

even the best wine turns to vinegar
if left to open air

all the most beautiful flowers
still wither
without the attention of the sun

I ask myself -
what could possibly spoil happiness
except focusing on the fact
that it may one day disappear?

I must face this love
dead or alive
no matter the consequence
no matter the wrath it may bring

BEAUTY TO BURN

The rose garden burns
with brief
and triumphant beauty

bursting forth
from silent meditation
revealing its soul to the sunlight
laying bear its essence

the rose puts in no extra effort
it just is and so shall be
a spontaneous and ancient seduction
a sudden and powerful enchantment

then again
isn't all beauty -
temporary?

a flicker in time
a moment held still
a thing to worship
beyond yourself

we all need this
something to strife towards
to be engulfed by

I needed this
your beauty more than any other
to be swallowed up in
to be enslaved by

to die in

SICK WITH OBSESSION

Smashed and Smeared
against the rocks of your shore
my blood for your attention
It is your gaze that I adore
I am but a drowned man
in the sea of your certainty

Bound and Gagged
more flesh thrown into love's device
Transmutations of the heart
from a wasted life - to sacred sacrifice
Allow me to feed and fuel
your furnace of desire

Entombed and Doomed
in saccharine bliss you capture
like insects in golden amber
all these moments are pure rapture
The orchid of my affection
shall never ever decay

Surfing and Suffering
because love is the ultimate whore
the paradox of necessity
eventually we all fall in this endless war
I am sick with obsession
but the cure and the poison
are one and the same

LEAVE A SCAR

It's the kiss that leaves a scar
sex that burns straight through - like a falling star

It's the memories that cannot be erased
 a story of blood and soul that we chased

Give me hell *and* high water
with Cupid's poisoned arrows
bring me to slaughter

A day without love's sorrow
is a day with no tomorrow

A life without love's passion
is one left colorless and ashen

Give me death and one last wish
keep your promise and make
my heart your fetish

All my reasons have been crucified
now I hang here in surrender – purified

Our bodies have merged like a total eclipse
as fate comes rushing to meet our eager lips

ALL OR NOTHING

Feed the dragon of curiosity -
endlessly
swim against the waves of certainty -
infinitely

(we must) believe that what's coming
is different than
what came before

we run in place
we push when it pulls
we are but reflections in mirrors
imprisoned in ever more mirrors

is the universe growing
or just becoming?
is there more matter
or just more space to occupy?

have we gained a thing at all
or has our perception changed?
our memories rearranged

happiness is a temporal delusion
suffering a similar illusion

knowledge in a vacuum
that cannot be filled
love is a trap
where nothing gets out alive

PAGAN PAGEANTRY

Enough time has passed now
fallen into the ruins of memory
much of my soul lies beneath
stains/ashes/and improbable weight

So much has come undone
been unraveled and forgotten
what remains has all but
surrendered/collapsed/been lulled to sleep

Nothing shall transpire anymore
without a fit of pageantry
without a thrashing and writhing
all too aware of its extinction

The once vibrant dream
dissolves like morning dew
revealing the wreckage
and the seed for a new nightmare

Spontaneity kisses nostalgia
but she never kisses back
only teases and plays her little tricks
from her prison of the past

I say, "Enough is Enough!"
as my cup overflows with white vinegar
as all the old scars ache to be reborn
as the candle in my heart spits hot wax

What is left of me
persists against all odds
like a primrose blooming in the moonlight
upon a grave without a name

SCALES

One day everything resides in its proper place
and you feel like you are "winning"
the charm comes easy
the laughter bursts forth
you want for nothing-more
than what you already hold

Then the next day comes
and you are suddenly wounded - bleeding out
your eyes sink back into their caves
the abysmal silence takes hold
watching as the bouquet of flowers
wilts within your heart

There are days when I can capture a perfect buzz
floating at the pinnacle of love's intoxication
the appetites stand wet and ready
ancient promises are fulfilled
every one of her curves - illuminated
and my hands can bring only pleasure

Then tomorrow comes to balance the scales
to remind me of the thorns upon the rose
the clouds cover the warmth of the sun
minds change and retreat
all that was right and true
begins to dissolve into regret

Must it be this way?
Has it always been this way?
Such a wretched creature I have become
praying to doomed gods to modify my fate
to leave the lynchpin of love in its place
to allow me to stay in that sacred space

Hell is a beautiful woman
who no longer cares

LOVE'S INSANITY

I have let the iron of my soul
decay and rust
my heart swells
with stagnant pools of lust

I asked oblivion to enter me
and name its place
to bring that strange and terrible color
from outer space

Coveting a fleeting peace
that we found in a cacophonous peak
we fucked like demons
on alters of God's made weak

Drinking down a shrinking universe
in translucent 3 oz. pours
I ate you and you ate me
becoming each other's whores

Dancing in love's insanity
beneath the moonlight
we freed our passions
but gave them endless appetite

I kneel before your sweet memory
broken and chained
yearning fills me like a chalice of blood
that cannot be drained

PROMETHEUS UNBOUND

I hold a box of wooden soldiers
lined up with readied attention

I fantasize about the dreams
locked inside their skulls

I gaze deep into
their red sulfurous minds

and wish to free
the potential locked therein

I raise up this future radiance
and I understand an exit

Kissing the lips of Prometheus
I give you a paradise of flames - *unbound*

PAIN OF PERFECTION

overwhelmed with love
it spews from every pore
swells up in my guts and
bursts from my chest

mauled by gratitude
it invades every neuron
rages in my bloodstream and
gushes off my tongue

destroyed by beauty
it entombs my every cell
purified in each breath
I am consumed by

the pain
of your patient
perfection

THE COPPER POT

For years we would write down fond memories of things that
made us happy or laugh.
Inside jokes, intimate moments, adventures, all the little things.
We would write them on thin scraps of paper.
Fold them up and put them in a small thrift store copper pot.
Over time they really piled up – threatening to spill over the
edge.

Then randomly or if we just needed a little reminder of our love.
We would each plunge our fingers in the pot and pull out a
memory.
Reading it aloud to each other and reveling in our fortune.
There were no bad selections. Everyone a banger.
It was a nice metaphor for the bulk of our relationship.
The overflowing cup.

Then one day, it all came to an end. The day arrived when she
broke it off with me.
We both went through a roller coaster of emotions. I was devas-
tated with sorrow.
And in a fit of denial and desperation –
I grabbed our sacred copper pot from the shelf
and enthusiastically emptied its contents into the air.
Over her head - sitting still in the bed.

They all came fluttering down - like sad confetti.
A hundred slivers of time where everything was right and well in
the world.
A hundred captured moments that refuse to be erased.
Like beautiful exotic birds - shot dead with a few simple words.
"I don't want this"

They landed all over the room. Surrounding us.
As if the last seven years had just exploded into our faces.
And in a way – now it had – quite literally.

I didn't intend for it to be so poetic. I just sort of did it.
An animal caught in a trap - howling out.
Like are you sure? What about all this!?

And I know that was only a fraction of the depth we shared.
Of the connection that remained.

If we shared the that much love -
in that quantity - for so long - how could it possibly just *vanish*?
Vaporize like some casual fling.
My heart just refuses to believe it. That it was temporary.

I know only this –
I don't want to fill yet another copper pot
with anyone else.

AT THE GATES

I've scrolled far past the doom
and now I sit in a vast empty room

A vacancy of utter dread
one in which I carelessly fed

Minutes into hours - hours into days
there is no exit in seems to this maze

A sea of humans speaking and dancing
yet silence drowns out all my advancing

How did we come to this state of human being
if seems with each photo we were agreeing

With each click we purchased our fates
and just like that we stand at the gates

A hell where the agony is isolation not fire
desensitized we have numbed all our desire

We've scrolled and scrolled far beyond doom
we've missed the peak of our life in bloom

Down into the valley of regret we go
deep into the river of night we shall row

WILD OATS

Reduced to rubble
fragments
of memories

moments
pleading
for new life

An agonizing wish
suffocated by
misunderstandings

A kiss
just inches
from paradise

reduced to ashes
and cold embers
of simple reveries

Hearts
craving
new cavities

a terrible secret
kept for too long
and buried too deep

a truth
so close
to being set free

"That maybe *love* - is not enough"

STAIN-GLASS HEART

I watch her bend down
to pick up the pieces
of my fragile glass heart
rearranging them into complex collages
of pain - of love - of obsession
so serene - so severe - so stunning
even when she can't stand me
I find her absolutely gorgeous

all that effort -
just to break apart
once more

I can hear the fiends - the bastards
the jackals of opportunity
behind every door
they creep and lurk
but mostly they plot and snicker
waiting for my demise -
for our collapse

with all of love's certainty
and yet still -
hell awaits

I observe these desperate lovers
wandering aimless
into downtown streets
into empty houses - into the abyss
just begging for their fates
to greet their dreams
to finally meet their maker

How much of this is choice
or within our control?

How many grains of sand
plummet
without notice
into the bottom of the hourglass?

We can no longer decipher
the dogs from the wolves
the angels from the devils
everything has hooves
a motive - an escape – an excuse
everything - everywhere
just some kind of abuse
we hold tight to reason
but just as much to whim

What if *true love*
is more about maintenance -
than circumstance?

My pillow has become a graveyard
of dead memories - of stale irises
a tomb - for all my aborted intentions
ones that will never again see the light

the sheets covered in stains
from all these tired tears
stains in the shape of could have been(s) – all most(s)
but never to be(s)

DEATH AND ANGELS

For some it's a splendid sculpture
perfectly posed in a marbled gallery
for others it's just the next cigarette
and a safe place to rest their head

You can find it after a strenuous hike
past the pines and up the mountain top
yet it also flickers in dying neon lights
and shifts between each roll of the die

Sometimes it appears in the throes of passion
excreted in molecules of sweat and cum
but it also emerges in the vacuum of solitude
as if it had always been there from the start

Often its where you least expect it to be
after a hard fall to your hands and knees
when you're flat broke and out of touch
in the depths of madness or heartbreak

there it waits -
forgiveness

Death always looks beautiful
if you know –
just how to hold the mirror

DECORATION

This is a message in a bottle
a white flag
a death without dying

This is a declaration
a sort of last breath – held forever
a kiss on the lips of a tombstone
hemlock to the spirt of love

I loved you
I love you
I'll always love you

All of you
every molecule
every mistake
every curve and freckle
every critique

But there was nothing left
to fight for
or against
that you hadn't
already won

I was just temporary –
something for awhile
ephemeral
a seasonal decoration
a plaything in time

But I hope you know
I want you to know
you must know

It felt like so much more

something immortal
something unbreakable
something untethered

My heart still lingers
on every word
written or hidden
spoken or transmitted
whispered or screamed

My soul is yet captured
by this little game

EXPIRED MOLECULES

Beauty
is a destroyer
of all our preconceptions
of our arrogance
and assuredness

it makes fools
of even the most
tyrannical

Nature
is a devourer
of all of our progress
of the noble
and wretched alike

it matters not
what importance in life
it will degrade and fade

Death
is just recycling
of expired molecules
of ancient designs
and tired ideas

we are swallowed by time
and spit back out
into a trillion tiny worlds

GLASCOW SMILE

Gutted -
by immaculate beauty

Eviscerated -
with a radiant touch

Cut from ear to ringing ear
with a knife of singing fear

Nothing -
shall ever be the same

All is twisted
and rearranged

The porcelain innocence of love
smashed to dust with a shove

Descending -
from supreme heights

Ascending -
to the hell of regret

Serenity ripped from the heart
in this wasteland we remain apart

DIE BY THE DROP

No more handouts
from grace

No more excess
without consequence

Every moment passing -
paid like a bill

The snakes of destiny
have all slithered home
to reclaim the dust

Without the sun
the moon gasps
and flickers out

I am face to face
with a living ghost

Drop by little drop -
I disappear

EDGE OF RAPTURE

And so it comes round again
the rusty nail lodged in the great wheel
a cigarette burn in the film of your memories
a blanket of white death upon the lilac bush

to remind us of our impermanence
to erase the progress of a burning season
to ensure we remain humble
upon the edge of rapture

a sort of perennial sadness
a kind of cyclical sorrow
it flows like temporal blood out of
every autumn chrysanthemum

You begin to ask yourself questions
that once seemed absurd
about purpose and surrender
about circumstance and limits

There must always be a test of integrity
for all valuable things
a tempering through heat and hammer
a gauntlet to eliminate the impurities

there will always remain resistance
against the hardest things in life
but it is this same resistance that
gives our essence its form

only on the other side
will quality be revealed
only upon exiting
can it be understood

only through metamorphosis
can anything truly become
its true self

AS ABOVE SO BELOW

I'll tell you what man
there is no such thing as a vacation
only moments strung together
love and death bound in desperation

Some of us have our hands out
begging for real change
others got their arms up in the sky
looking totally deranged

Maybe one of these days
I'll stop caring about the truth
until then I'll be right here
fighting nail and fucking tooth

Meaning locked inside tragedy
pain and wisdom - tit for tat
this life is a comedy of errors
but it's a sick joke we can all laugh at

Come what may
the problem lies in the trying
as above so below
the feelings leave with the crying

Never a right time only passing seconds
sand shifting to make more room
chaos keeping the rhythm alive
from womb to bittersweet tomb

REMEMBER TO BREATHE

My days drip slowly away
like wax from a candle
and in the flickering light
I dared to hope
that we could change
that I would change in time

I genuflect on the ruins
of all my expectations
and spit into the ashes
of incinerated angels

I know deep in my heart
there is no such thing
as *nothing*
not anymore

Every inhale - A new universe
Each exhale - A Swan's Song

beauty remains frozen
in the eye of my destroyer

my freedom is captured
on tongue of my redeemer

truth is a slave
dancing in chains

beneath this absurd armor
is a wounded child

when this love is exhausted
there will be nothing left to conquer
only one thing remains –
to surrender once more

DISINTEGRATE

Exiled from myself
from culture
from purpose
Exiled from wanting any more

Into the void I am cast
toward the exit I am thrown

The single truth I know
is that only the *present* exists

Only a razor thin moment
on the move

Oscillating between a
crumbling past and
some eventual apocalypse

Never quite enough
Never quite content

The true prize dancing
in magnetic movement -
just keep moving

One must slurp up the
melting moment

Lick up the dust of
all that came before

Can we unweave hubris
From our passion?

Can we strip control
from our obsession?

If you blink you just might
miss the love that escaped
went running for the hills

If you wait too long
all you thought was real
will disintegrate into the past

BEGGAR KING

I sit here once again
cold, empty, abandoned
by love
by her
by fate

and yet I go on - like a fool
or maybe a desperate soldier
who things something - someone
waits for him

to return *home*
for a kiss
a cold beer
a chance at a fresh start

but it is all a prayer
a plead to vacant clouds
that do not listen - nor hear

It is all a sort of gamble
that it might get better
that your best days are not
already behind you

the scales of life
weighing down the heart –
drowning the soul
in their indifferent hands

Some nights I am the angel
with wings clipped singing
sad songs with the morning birds

Some nights I am a demon
with a restless heart
feeding an endless fire

but most nights –
I but a beggar
stalking the lonely streets
asking for coins and attention

a strange man with a tall tale
of how - "once upon a time"
I was king of the universe

MUSEUM

I pace around this beautiful
yet hollow house

it's filled with nice things
that are rarely used -
barely touched

a museum now
of something past
of something lost

I catch glimpses of my stoic face
I see the grey hairs creeping
across my beard like slow fire

I see little lines emerging under
my eyes and upon my brow
and not enough in my cheeks

I make an extravagant dinner
for *one*
in theory it's delicious and nutritious
but somehow - it's not

some critical ingredient
has gone missing
and in a way
I guess that's what life is now

on the surface
all well and good
but deep down inside
the most
important thing

just isn't there

THE HALF-EMPTY BED

Each morning - upon awakening
the mind has forgotten
albeit temporarily –
all that came before

the details
exactly what the world is
and no longer is
(the dreamer) has become
a brief *tabula rasa*

As tired eyes crack open
they look across the bed
in search of her warm body
but she is no longer there

hands reach
for the elegant curve of her hips
finding only crumpled blanket and thin air
a heart driven back into despair

memories flood
seeking purchase to live again
finding only a vast and empty space
vacancy without a trace

As if eternally waking
into a circular nightmare
I can't help but hope
to continue sleeping
or once again open my eyes
to hers staring back

NO REST FOR THE WICKED

Where did you sleep last night?
I guess it doesn't matter. Not anymore.
It no longer matters
that someone still waits for you to come home.
That someone still feels bound
like so much threadbare yarn
around a heart fated to burst.

Where did you sleep last night?
It's as if monogamy was just a game.
Something for the old and tired.
For the settled or complacent.
A trap for the one who stays in-love longer.
While the other remains free and unbound
by weight or gravity. The wild one.

Where did you sleep last night?
It's as if love is now but a joke for the unrequited. The reject-
ed.
A slow methodical punchline.
And yet finding the laughter remains elusive no matter the
effort.
The actual answer is unimportant. It will not bring peace.
It cannot bring back the beautiful thing dead upon the alter.
Cannot put back the pieces of what was shattered.

RETURN BY FIRE

Doom has arrived
to replace the cavity
that love left behind
like so much soot and ash
after the volcano has erupted

A deep vacancy is felt
alive in every pore
as if each cell of my body
is missing something vital -
essential to its purpose

I carry on
like a limp marionette
dancing to a lifeless beat
smiling with slow
mechanized effort

They say loss is an opportunity
to learn and to grow
somehow this is feeble medicine
to the gaping wounds
of paradise lost

Come Father Time
with all your severity
and harsh wisdom
come wash me with absentia -
give me back to the cosmos

anguish -
is the only thing I have left
that I can still call my own

sorrow –
is what remains
of her radiant glow

LOVE'S PERSISTENCE

These wars within
are everything
they provide the fire
that tempers our pride
they are the blade
that trims away our greed

they come to balance the scales
destroying all that doesn't belong

In the embers of our struggles
we reveal the steel of truth
beneath the fat of excess and luxury
lies our true selves

when nothing else remains
only then shall we understand
what *freedom* is

Gourmands of each other's heart
we could eat for eternity
and never be satiated
starved to the brink of death
we would survive on just the chance
that love could push us through

Our only true victory in life
is finally surrendering
to love's persistence

IT'S JUST A RIDE

Exhaustion screams
from my bloodshot eyes
Ennui drips down
from an artificial smile

Passion explodes and then dies
in continuously waves -
everything - in fits and starts

My heart is an engine
left out in the rain – sputtering
eons seem to pass in a flash

My deepest gratitude
always followed - by a strange regret
in spiraling loops

I'm just along for the ride –
but it's a ride I don't remember buying the ticket for
a ride I can't seem to get off of

It's summertime
and I take this opportunity
to look briefly - but directly
into the mighty sun
it is a god after all

A tangible and honest one
my god is the sun
until I move on into molecule spray
and mycelia decay

Sitting beneath the full glory
of summer's power
here in the land of four seasons
where the soul is always sick

yet habitually healing
resurrecting into its next form

The autumn is out there
quietly slumbering until its time comes
but for now - it is summer
and this sweltering heat reminds me
of extremis
of transitions
of sex and death
of catharsis
and consequence

Summer provides -
it gives and gives like some machine gone mad
Summer doesn't beg or demand
it demonstrates
with undeniable conviction

Summer is here
and she is not
She is elsewhere
basking under god's glorious rays
without me – apart from me

Lonely has never been the right word
to capture her absentia
never strong enough
never complete enough

Something parasitic eats my thoughts
consuming them for their own device
Something is burning up my soul
using me like fuel to run its engine of sorrow

This is a poem about having everything
you could possibly need under the sun
and still something is missing

A poem about drinking from a full cup -
and yet always feeling drained

As if every sacred eucharist
is just one more stale cracker

To have loved and lost
is like being buried alive
laid into a coffin –
made from your own skin
and pound shut with iron nails

but god shines on
helpless or indifferent
it's always hard to tell

FORGOTTEN PROPHET

I leave behind these memories
like so many orphans into the street

they are wet from the rain of my tears
soaked in meaning and contradiction

vigorous love dances with profound anguish
intense passion marionets alongside loathing

I leave behind my precious words
like so many unread books upon the shelf

a few I have written and many more collected
but all are stained with her sweet perfume

such fragile little things
barely able to escape the tip of my tongue

I abandon these glorious moments
like stillborn creatures not fully formed

trapped forever in darkness and silence
a lifetime of searching
only to release your greatest treasure –
back into the sea

a heart as heavy as an *anchor*
sinking to the ocean floor
with all the beauty it has beheld

EMBERS

"I didn't mean to break you" she said
with her steady voice in something close to amusement
that coy and alluring tone

I looked up at her with eyes drained of tears
replaced and filled by growing fears
knowing full well that I was beyond broken
I was completely devastated and shattered
a pathetic mosaic of 10,000 pieces upon the floor

With her swift and cunning certainty
she had retired our love to the street
in a sudden crescendo - heart meets concrete
like a guillotine with a dull blade
made me a thing of her past

And so I am forced to ask -
What is Love?
if not something to fight for
protect and defend against all predators
even each other's trappings

What is Love?
If not something to fall towards
dive into completely
no matter the consequences

Love is a flickering fire
sometimes it rages and illuminates without fail
sometimes it dims - going quiet and pale

you can be sure if it was ever there to begin with
all it takes is a well-placed kiss
an honest rush of playful bliss

it will come alive once more

catching everything up in its pyre
all the more when we feed its desire

but a choice was made
to piss upon the coals that held the light
that still refused to give up the sacred fight
potential covered
truth smothered

another fire elsewhere was chosen to tend
but that's just life huh? - let's not pretend
another heart selected to ignite and extinguish
to build up and then snuff out with slow anguish

Yet still I shall remain *here*
beneath the fire's full collapse
blowing on the tiniest of embers
praying like a sinner for the relapse

IT'S AT THE BOTTOM

Now is the time to rejoice!
in the center of the maelstrom
at the zenith of annihilation
before the inevitable
has taken shape

Genuflect in the ruins
of all that came before
howl at celestial bodies
that still hang in their cradles
of fusion and fire

Drain your vessel
of every last tear
and all of its laughter -
so that the meaning
may resurface

Slit the wrist of resistance
and wait patiently
as the full contents
of sorrow manifests
and blooms with purpose

Sometimes it takes disaster
to reveal the gratitude below
Sometimes it requires love's fury
to give the ego its deathblow

Atropos

FINAL POEM

there is no ultimate poem
no eulogy to recite
no epitaph upon the stone

there is nothing left to say
only observe these moments
expiring all the time

there can be no last poem
no miracle that gives us wings
no escape from fate's fine thread

there are no correct words to utter
only a manuscript written in atoms
left for oblivion's appetite

there shall be no final poem
no sword held against destiny's desire
no love that can alter death's wish

there is only a final kiss to the stars
suspended in the air like a hummingbird
pleading for - ever more nectar

Amore Fatigue
by
Ryan Morrow